WANTED!

— FAMOUS OUTLAWS —

BILLY THE KID

A NOTORIOUS GUNFIGHTER OF THE WILD WEST

TIM COOKE

 Gareth Stevens
PUBLISHING

Please visit our website, **www.garethstevens.com**.
For a free color catalog of all our high-quality books,
call toll-free 1-800-542-2595 or fax 1-877-542-2596.

Library of Congress Cataloging-in-Publication Data

Cooke, Tim, 1961- author.
Billy the Kid : a notorious gunfighter of the wild west / Tim Cooke.
    pages cm. — (Wanted! Famous outlaws)
Includes index.
ISBN 978-1-4824-4243-4 (pbk.)
ISBN 978-1-4824-4244-1 (6 pack)
ISBN 978-1-4824-4245-8 (library binding)
1. Billy, the Kid—Juvenile literature. 2. Outlaws—Southwest, New—Biography—Juvenile literature.
3. Southwest, New—Biography—Juvenile literature. I. Title.
F786.B54C64 2016
364.15'52092—dc23
[B]
                              2015027021

Published in 2016 by
Gareth Stevens Publishing
111 East 14th Street, Suite 349
New York, NY 10003

For Brown Bear Books Ltd:
Editorial Director: Lindsey Lowe
Managing Editor: Tim Cooke
Children's Publisher: Anne O'Daly
Design Manager: Keith Davis
Designer: Melissa Roskell
Picture Manager: Sophie Mortimer

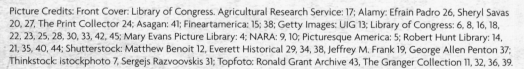

Manufactured in the United States of America
CPSIA compliance information: Batch #CW16GS. For further information contact Gareth Stevens, New York, New York at 1-800-542-2595.

CONTENTS

INTRODUCTION

Billy the Kid became famous as a gunfighter in the West. It was said that he shot more than 20 men dead. Despite this, he was very popular with people who knew him.

Billy's real name was William Henry McCarty. He was later also known as William H. Bonney. He is thought to have been born on November 23, 1859, and lived in the West at a time when there were few **sheriffs**. Many people carried guns to defend themselves or to hunt with. Even at a time when guns were common, Billy was famous for being a ruthless killer.

Hunters bring food back to a home on the frontier. Many settlers in the West lived in isolated places where there were no laws.

The Wild West

By 1840, nearly seven million Americans had moved from the East to settle west of the Appalachian Mountains. The land these settlers claimed had been occupied for centuries by Native Americans. There were many clashes between settlers and native tribes.

In 1846, the United States went to war with Mexico. After US victory in 1848, American territory increased to include Mexican land in what is now California and the Southwest. When gold was found in California in 1849, the number of pioneers heading west quickly increased.

This picture shows pioneers traveling in a wagon train. Thousands of people from the East followed wagon trails to the West in the hopes of making a new life.

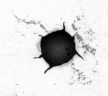

Sheriffs Officials whose job it is to enforce laws and arrest lawbreakers.

On the railroads

Some people headed west in the hopes of making a fortune. Others just wanted to claim some land to farm. Large-scale westward expansion was made possible by the building of the railroads. By 1860, railroads spread a third of the way across the United States. The railroads carried settlers into the West. As the railroads grew, so did the number of small towns and settlements along the line.

Towns sprung up in a random way. They started with cabins made from **adobe** or logs. Then came larger houses and stores to sell supplies. Services such as hotels and schools followed. Law and order was usually one of the last things to arrive. The US Army had forts in important places, but huge areas

were policed only by sheriffs and their deputies. Often, settlers were responsible for enforcing the law themselves. Disputes occurred when different people claimed the same piece of land. Ranchers wanted to graze their herds on the **range**. They were angry when farmers fenced off pieces of land. The disputes often ended in violent clashes. Some ranchers hired gunmen for protection. One of those gunmen was Billy the Kid.

Billy the Kid spent most of his life in New Mexico, living as a cowboy on the open range or in small towns.

Adobe Bricks made from mud dried in the sun.

Range An open area of land where livestock can wander and graze.

Irish Roots

Billy's early life remains a mystery. Historians know some of the story, but many facts are missing.

Some experts think this photograph shows Billy at the age of about 18 years old.

Historians believe that Billy was born William Henry McCarty in New York City in 1859. His mother was an Irishwoman named Catherine McCarty. She moved with Billy and his brother, Joseph, to Indiana in around 1868. There is no record of Billy's father.

A devoted son

Billy was devoted to his mother. Catherine did people's laundry and sold food to make money. She sent her boys to school, so they learned to read and write. They later moved to Wichita, Kansas. In 1873 Catherine married William Antrim. By then she was sick with **tuberculosis**. The family moved again to the mining town of Silver City, New Mexico. They hoped the dry climate would help Catherine's health. A year later, Catherine was dead.

This photograph of Fort Wingate, New Mexico, shows the kind of small town that was scattered across the territory.

Billy was devastated by Catherine's death. His stepfather disappeared, and Billy and Joseph were looked after by a woman named Mrs. Truesdell. For the next year, Billy worked in Truesdell's hotel. He was just 15 years old. While working at the hotel, Billy befriended a thief known as Sombrero Jack. Many people think Billy's life of crime was the result of a bad choice of friends in his youth.

SOMBRERO JACK

Sombrero Jack got his nickname from the Mexican hat he wore. His real name was George Schaefer. Jack got Billy into trouble after Jack robbed a Chinese laundry. He persuaded Billy to take the blame. It was Billy's first brush with the law.

Tuberculosis An infectious disease that attacks the lungs and makes it difficult to breathe.

Billy's First Victim

Billy was jailed after getting into trouble with the law in Silver City, but he escaped and left New Mexico for Arizona.

This photograph shows Fort Grant, Arizona, in about 1871.

Over the next two years, Billy moved around Arizona. In the spring of 1876, he stole a horse and headed for Fort Grant. In town, he took any work he could find as a cowboy or a cook. He also began gambling to raise money. When he had saved enough, he bought himself a **revolver**.

At Fort Grant, Billy met a local criminal named John Mackie. Mackie taught Billy how to steal horses. Billy became a skilled **rustler**. Soon, however, Mackie and Billy were caught. They were sent to jail, but Billy soon escaped. He was famous throughout his life for his ability to get out of jail.

Death of a bully

Billy was quickly recaptured by the local blacksmith, Frank "Windy" Cahill. Cahill was a big man who had often taken pleasure in bullying Billy. Billy was an easy target because of his slim build. Billy went back to prison but escaped again.

In August 1877, Cahill attacked Billy for the last time. After pushing Billy to the floor, Cahill sat on him and began to hit him. Billy managed to draw his gun from its holster. He shot Cahill at close range. Cahill died the next day. Billy fled. He was now a wanted murderer and an outlaw.

"THE KID"

It was in Fort Grant that Billy started to be known as "the Kid." Most people think he was given the nickname because he looked so young. He was also short and slim, so he appeared younger than he was.

These cattle rustlers wear masks to hide their faces in case they are recognized.

Revolver A pistol with a revolving chamber to hold bullets.

Rustler Someone who steals cattle or horses.

Focus: The Wild West

Billy lived at a time when the West was changing. But its popular image as a lawless place was kept alive.

Many myths grew up about life in the Wild West One popular story was that there was no law and order. It was said that people in the West settled disputes using their guns.

Guns in the West

However, while most men in the West carried a gun, gunfights were rare. More often ranchers hired cowboys who knew how to use a gun in order to protect their valuable cattle from rustlers. Native Americans also continued to be a threat to settlers, who carried guns to protect themselves. If gunfights did take place, they were usually caused by land disputes or **feuds** between families.

Frontier towns often passed laws forbidding men from carrying guns on the streets. The local sheriff could take their weapons. Despite

By the 1870s, there were more sheriffs in the West. The enforcement of law and order was becoming more commonplace.

such laws, many Americans still believed what they read about the West. Cheap **dime novels** were popular across the country. They created the image of the West as a place without laws. After Billy became famous, stories about him appeared in many dime novels. They usually described him as being a lone gunfighter. In fact, Billy spent most of his life as a cowboy working on the range.

SIX-SHOOTERS

The most popular gun in the West was the Colt .45 revolver. The gun was also called a six-shooter because its chamber held six bullets. The gun fit into a holster on the hip. The Colt .45 is sometimes called "the gun that won the West."

Many stories that were written about Billy the Kid had no connection with actual events in his life.

Feuds Long and bitter quarrels.

Dime novels Cheap, popular books that usually tell very romantic or dramatic stories.

Cattle Rustler

After the murder of Frank Cahill, Billy fled back to New Mexico where he continued his life of crime.

This was the home of the rancher John Chisum in Lincoln County. Billy's gang stole Chisum's cattle.

Billy returned briefly to Silver City, but did not stay long. Instead, he headed to the open range. He survived with the help of Mexicans who were living there. Billy spoke good Spanish and was popular with local Hispanics wherever he went.

Joining The Boys

Billy joined a gang of rustlers known as "The Boys." They were led by Jesse Evans. Evans had worked for a well-known rancher named John Chisum, in Lincoln County. The Boys were one of the most active cattle-rustling gangs in New Mexico. They **terrorized** ranchers and local residents in Doña Ana

County. When local lawmen began to catch up with them, the gang rode on to Lincoln County. They began stealing Chisum's cattle.

An easy crime

Stealing cattle was illegal but it was easy because the herds grazed on the open range. Armed cowboys did manage to stop some rustlers, but gangs stole cattle at night. It was often days before the theft was noticed. By then the cattle and the rustlers were long gone.

Cowboys round up cattle on the range. The cattle herds were so big rustlers often stole cows without being noticed.

BILLY'S MANY NAMES

After joining The Boys, Billy changed his name. He had been known as Billy Antrim, which was his stepfather's name. Now he became William Bonney. Why he chose the name is not known. At different times, Billy went by Billy Antrim, Kid Antrim, William Bonney, and The Kid. He only became known as Billy the Kid at the end of his life.

Terrorized Caused someone to feel fear and terror.

Focus: The Ranchers

The coming of the railroads meant that there was a huge amount of money to be made from raising cattle in the West and transporting them to the East.

Ranchers and their families lived in large, isolated homes. Their cowboys lived in a bunkhouse nearby.

Cattle ranching began in Texas in the 1820s. The ranches were run by Mexican cowboys known as *vaqueros*. In 1836, Texas became **independent** from Mexico. Texan ranchers drove out the Mexicans and kept the cattle. During the Civil War (1861–1865), the cattle roamed free and the herds grew. At the end of the war, the Texans rounded up the cattle and drove them north to sell. The railroads carried cattle to feed people in the cities of the East.

Modern cowboys still drive cattle across the range. Herds are a fraction of the size they once were.

Expanding into New Mexico

John Simpson Chisum (1824–1884) was one of the first ranchers to send herds into New Mexico territory. He built up herds of around 100,000 cattle. They grazed on land he held by "right of discovery." This allowed settlers to claim unoccupied land in the West. Chisum hired armed cowboys to protect his cattle from rustlers. When the cattle were ready for market, cowboys drove them north to the railroads. The railroads took the animals to **railheads** such as Chicago, where they were killed for beef.

COW TOWNS

Towns sprang up along the cattle trails that led to the railroads. These were called cow towns. They supplied the cowboys who drove the cattle. A typical cow town had places to sleep and eat. There were saloons where men drank and gambled away their earnings. A general store sold all kinds of supplies.

Independent Governing itself.

Railheads Towns where railroads join important roads or trails.

A New Family

Billy quit cattle rustling sometime around October 1877 when a chance meeting changed his life.

The Apache of New Mexico sometimes attacked white settlers on their land.

According to one story, Billy the Kid was on his own on the range when an Apache stole his horse. Native Americans sometimes ambushed white settlers and stole from them. Without his horse, Billy walked miles. He suffered from lack of food and water. He was close to death when he reached a farm owned by Heiskell Jones. Barbara, Jones' wife, was known for her good food and hospitality. The Joneses had a large family. They welcomed Billy into their home.

Billy's stay at the Jones' farm came at a good time. While he was there, the past caught up with Jesse Evans. The leader of The Boys was captured after a gun battle and put in the Lincoln County jail.

Looking for work

Barbara Jones took care of Billy. When he recovered his health, the family gave him one of their horses. Billy went to look for work in Lincoln County. He rode into a tense situation. A friend of John Chisum wanted to start a ranch in Lincoln County. Chisum was backing him. However, local businessmen were determined to stop him.

Heiskell Jones and his family lived in the Pecos Valley of New Mexico.

THE COUNTY SEAT

Lincoln County was the same size as South Carolina, but it only had 2,000 residents. The main town was Lincoln City. Only 400 people lived there. The main street was lined with one-story, adobe-brick buildings. The town's only two-story building was the general store. The county jail opened in 1877. It was just a hole in the ground with a guard cabin.

Hospitality The friendly treatment of guests, visitors, or strangers.

Death of John Tunstall

Billy was soon in trouble in Lincoln County. This time, his horse rustling had an unexpected result.

Billy tried to steal horses from a rancher named John Tunstall. Tunstall was an Englishman who had moved to Lincoln County with his friend, an attorney named Alexander McSween. John Chisum had helped Tunstall buy a ranch. When Tunstall caught Billy stealing his horses, he did not send him to jail. Instead, he hired Billy to work for him.

Taking on The House

As a member of The Boys, Billy had rustled cattle for a rancher named Jimmy Dolan. Dolan was part of a group of citizens known as the House. They ran

Much of Lincoln County was open, bleak land. Huge areas of the territory were uninhabited.

John Tunstall was said to have been shot after he surrendered to three of Brady's deputies.

Lincoln County as if they owned it. The House wanted Tunstall to leave town. Sheriff William Brady worked for the House. He sent a **posse** to Tunstall's ranch with a fake **court order** to seize Tunstall's property.

On February 18, 1878, Tunstall and his men, including Billy the Kid, rode into town to challenge the court order. On the way they met Brady's posse. Tunstall was gunned down. His murder brought the feud with the House to a head. This was now war.

JOHN TUNSTALL (1853-1878)

Born in England, John Tunstall wanted to make a fortune in the West. He used money given to him by his father to become a rancher and merchant in Lincoln County. He clashed with the largely Irish ranchers and merchants who ran the county. In the end, Tunstall paid with his life.

Posse A group of citizens helping a sheriff.

Court order An official order made by a judge or court.

Focus: Land Wars in the West

The struggle in Lincoln County was not the only violent clash in the West. The clashes were called land wars or range wars.

10. OPEN RANGE BRANDING.
COPYRIGHT 1904 BY C. R. KENDRICK, DENVER.

Cowboys round up cattle for **branding**. Ranchers wanted to keep land as open range for grazing their herds. Farmers wanted the land to grow crops.

Much of the land in the West did not officially belong to anyone. Ranchers claimed huge areas, known as the range, for grazing their cattle. Cowboys were hired by ranchers to protect their livestock. In some places, ranchers argued about who owned the land. In addition, ranchers sometimes tried to fight off settlers who tried to start **smallholdings** or farms on the range. These settlers were legally entitled to claim land to farm. But the ranchers were angry when the settlers fenced off parts of the range. That meant there was less space for the herds to roam.

Range wars

There were range wars in Johnson County, Wyoming, and Mason County, Texas. Dozens of people were killed. The ranchers could afford to hire cowboys, lawmen, and gunfighters. They behaved like private armies. The Lincoln County War was one of the most serious land wars. It was not just the ranchers and merchants who fought. Local lawmen took sides and the US government sent in the US Cavalry.

★★★ JOHNSON COUNTY WAR

In Johnson County, Wyoming, ranchers clashed with new settlers. In 1892, the ranchers hired around 50 gunmen. The gunmen invaded the county and killed opponents of the ranchers. The settlers and the local sheriff formed a posse of about 200 men. The two sides fought one another until the US Cavalry ended the war in 1893.

This cowboy was photographed in 1888. Ranchers hired cowboys who could use guns to defend their herds.

Branding The burning of an owner's identification mark on an animal's skin.

Smallholding A small property used for farming.

The Regulators

After John Tunstall was killed, Billy the Kid wanted to get revenge for his employer's death.

This photograph shows three lawmen in Lincoln County around the time of the war.

John Tunstall's friend, Alexander McSween, wanted to catch Tunstall's killers. He tried to persuade the authorities in Lincoln County to investigate the murder. That would mean investigating the House, the group led by Jimmy Dolan. However, The House controlled the sheriff. It was made clear there would be no investigation. Alexander McSween became scared for his own safety. He fled Lincoln County.

The Regulators

John Wilson was a local **justice of the peace**. He wanted to investigate Tunstall's murder and asked the foreman from Tunstall's ranch, Dick Brewer, to help. Wilson gave Brewer **warrants** to make arrests. Brewer formed a posse known as the Regulators. It numbered up to 60 men, including Billy the Kid. The posse also included many Mexican-Americans. They wanted to fight the House to end its control of the county.

This is the most famous photograph of Billy. It probably shows him in around 1879.

Another murder

The Regulators spent five months in Lincoln County hunting down Tunstall's murderers. Billy was the most loyal of the Regulators. He was the only member who was present at every one of the Regulators' gunfights.

In March 1878, the Regulators tracked down Buck Morton, the man who had shot Tunstall. Three days later, Morton was found dead with two other men. However, Sheriff Brady still refused to make any arrests in connection with Tunstall's murder. On April 1, 1878, six Regulators, including Billy, ambushed and killed Sheriff Brady on Lincoln's main street.

A STEP TOO FAR?

After John Tunstall's murder, many Lincoln residents supported the Regulators. They saw them as enforcing the law. The murder of Sheriff Brady changed that. Many residents decided the gang was just as bloodthirsty as the House.

Justice of the peace A local legal official with powers to investigate some crimes.

Warrants Documents authorizing an arrest.

The Battle of Lincoln

The shooting of Sheriff Brady started a period of even more violence in Lincoln County.

This wall painting shows Billy's friend, Tom O'Folliard. Tom rode with the Regulators.

The Regulators met and fought with Brady's posse at Blazer's Mill on April 4, 1878. The Regulators' leader, Dick Brewer, was shot dead. He was replaced by Frank McNab. Meanwhile the House decided that the sheriff who replaced Brady was too sympathetic to the Regulators. They forced him to **resign** and made George W. Peppin sheriff.

By now news of the violence had spread beyond Lincoln County. A unit of US Cavalry had arrived to enforce the law. They sided with Peppin and the men working for the House. The next battle took place in the town of Lincoln itself. The Regulators fought against Peppin's men and the cavalry, but they were outnumbered. Billy and the Regulators fled and hid in the countryside. A posse of House supporters was on their trail.

The Five-Day War

Billy and the Regulators spent a few weeks in hiding. In July 1878, Billy and a few others returned to Alexander McSween's home in Lincoln. The House discovered they were there. Their men surrounded the building. For four days the two sides exchanged gunfire. On the fifth day, Peppin's men set McSween's home on fire. Inside, Billy came up with an escape plan. He and the others fled out of the back door. Not everyone survived. McSween was shot dead as he tried to escape.

Billy and the Regulators spent weeks hiding in the countryside around Lincoln.

McSWEEN'S DEATH

The death of McSween marked the end of the feud between Tunstall's supporters and the House. With Tunstall and McSween both dead, there was no point in carrying on the feud. The House still ran Lincoln County.

Resign To voluntarily give up a job or an official position.

Amnesty Denied

After the escape from Lincoln, Billy became the leader of the Regulators. But he was also a wanted outlaw.

Governor Lew Wallace was also a writer. He wrote the best-selling novel *Ben Hur* (1880).

The Lincoln County War ended with McSween's death. In a few months, Billy had become famous. He was now the most wanted criminal in America's Southwest.

Amnesty

In September 1878, a new governor arrived in New Mexico Territory. Lew Wallace had been an officer in the Civil War. To try to bring peace to Lincoln County, Wallace offered an **amnesty** to anyone who had been involved in the land war, as long as they had not been charged with a crime. Billy was already wanted for two murders, so he was not offered amnesty. Billy decided to try another way. In February 1879, the House and the Regulators met. They agreed to stop killing each other. They also agreed not to act as witnesses against each other in court. The agreement did not last long. While drunk, one of the House posse shot dead Huston Chapman, a lawyer who had been a supporter of the Regulators.

Plea for immunity

In March 1879, Billy wrote to Governor Wallace. He asked for **immunity** from prosecution in return for acting as a witness against Jimmy Dolan and other House members. Wallace agreed. Billy was put in jail while he waited to give his evidence. However, the government decided to put him on trial for Sheriff Brady's murder. Billy knew he would not receive a fair trial so he escaped and went on the run again.

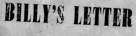

BILLY'S LETTER

Unlike many outlaws, Billy could read and write. He wrote a letter to Governor Lew Wallace. Billy offered to act as a witness against Jimmy Dolan. The letter shows that Billy was ready to stop the fighting.

This WANTED poster for Billy is a fake. It was created after Billy's death, when he had become famous. The amount of $5,000 in 1879 equals $110,000 today.

REWARD
($5,000.00)

Reward for the capture, dead or alive, of one Wm. Wright, better known as

"BILLY THE KID"

Age, 18. Height, 5 feet, 3 inches. Weight, 125 lbs. Light hair, blue eyes and even features. He is the leader of the worst band of desperadoes the Territory has ever had to deal with. The above reward will be paid for his capture or positive proof of his death.

JIM DALTON, Sheriff.

DEAD OR ALIVE!
"BILLY THE KID"

Amnesty An official pardon for a crime.

Immunity A promise that someone will not be punished for a crime.

The Empty Chamber

On the run, Billy spent the rest of 1879 rustling cattle. He also carried out one of his most famous killings.

Billy ended up living near the small town that grew up next to the army base at Fort Sumner.

Billy was living near Fort Sumner, a US Army base in southeastern New Mexico. He rustled from John Chisum's herds. He said the rancher owed him for the time Billy had spent fighting on the side of Tunstall and Chisum during the Lincoln County War.

A famous story

In January 1880 Billy killed a man named Joe Grant in a saloon in Fort Sumner. The murder became one of the most famous episodes of Billy's life. Grant was drinking heavily. He boasted that he would kill Billy the Kid. He did not know Billy was in the bar listening to him.

Deadly trick

As Grant became drunk, Billy asked if he could look at Grant's revolver. Billy secretly removed a bullet from the gun's **cylinder**. He rotated the cylinder so the hammer was above the empty chamber. Billy then revealed who he was to Grant and turned away. Grant reached for the gun and fired at Billy's back. The hammer fell on the empty chamber, so nothing happened. Billy then turned and shot Grant dead. It looked as though he had acted in self-defense.

A revolver fires when the trigger is pulled and the hammer inside the gun falls against a bullet held in the cylinder.

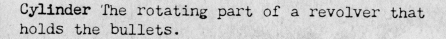

Cylinder The rotating part of a revolver that holds the bullets.

Focus: Gunfighters

Gunfighters are some of the most famous characters of the Wild West, but they are also some of the most often misunderstood.

The image of two gunfighters meeting in the street has been popular for over a century.

Billy the Kid was just one of the outlaws who became famous for his deadly skill with his gun. The buffalo hunter Bat Masterson and the Texan John Wesley Hardin were also feared gunfighters throughout the West. Other gunfighters became lawmen, such as Wild Bill Hickok and Wyatt Earp. These men were known for being quick to go for their guns. They were also good shots.

Western movies have created a misleading image of gunfighters. They suggest that gunfighters were **romantic** figures. They portray gunfights in

Modern Wild West reconstructions often include pretend gunfights.

which two enemies face each other on a dusty main street and race to pull out their guns. The loser ends up dead.

Disappearing gunmen

In reality, the real West never had as many gunfighters as the **fictionalized** stories suggest. They only existed from the end of the Civil War in 1865 until the 1880s. Most gunfights were short and confused. The enemies rarely faced each other in the open. Most were careful to take cover.

POLICE GAZETTE

Police Gazette was a popular magazine. It told dramatic stories of crime. *Police Gazette* began the myth of the gunfighter. Its stories of the West were read in saloons, barbershops, and pool halls. Each edition was passed from reader to reader until it fell apart. The accounts made gunfighters sound more romantic than they really were.

Romantic Associated with an idealized and perfect view of reality.

Fictionalized Describes true stories to which details have been added to turn them into fiction.

The Law Closes In

In November 1880 a man named Pat Garrett was elected sheriff of Lincoln County. Billy's luck was about to run out.

This picture shows Billy shooting a man who had pointed a gun at him. The incident probably never happened.

Pat Garrett had been a bartender. He was elected sheriff because he promised to catch rustlers and outlaws, including Billy the Kid.

Billy was wanted for his part in the Lincoln County War in 1878 and for three murders. Governor Wallace offered a $500 **reward** ($11,000 in today's money) for anyone who could catch or kill him.

Wanted man

Pat Garrett wanted to collect the reward for Billy. He organized a posse and set out to track Billy down. He caught up with Billy at Fort Sumner. Billy was leading a gang that had been stealing horses. It was winter, and Billy managed to escape from Garrett's posse during a snowstorm.

Pat Garrett later claimed to be good friends with Billy. In fact, they hardly knew each other.

A trap

Garrett decided to set a trap. He told people in Fort Sumner that his posse was turning back because of the snow. When the news reached Billy, he decided it was safe for the gang to return to Fort Sumner.

Billy and the rest of his gang returned to the town. They took refuge in an abandoned building that had once been a hospital. At around midnight on December 19, 1880, Garrett's posse attacked the hospital. A gunfight followed. Billy's friend Tom O'Folliard was killed. Billy and some of the others got away. Yet again, Billy the Kid was on the run from the law.

PAT GARRETT
(1850-1908)

Before he became sheriff of Lincoln County, Pat Garrett had a varied past. He had worked as a cowboy, buffalo hunter, trail driver, bartender, and hog raiser. He was said to have shot a fellow hunter dead in Texas. After that he left for New Mexico to open his own saloon.

Reward Money offered in return for the capture or killing of a wanted criminal.

Under Arrest

If it had not been for the betrayal of a friend or the body of a dead horse, Billy might not have been captured.

This picture shows the dead horse blocking the doorway of the outlaws' hideout.

On the run, Billy and his gang hid at the ranch of a friend named Manuel Brazil. But Brazil **betrayed** Billy. He told Pat Garrett where the outlaws were hiding. Believing that Garrett was back in Fort Sumner, the gang had gone to an abandoned stone building. It was in a place named Stinking Springs, because the plants around it smelled bad. As the outlaws slept inside the **hideout**, Garrett and his posse surrounded the tiny, windowless building. Early in the morning, one of the outlaws stepped out through the door. He was wearing a sombrero, like

Billy wore. No one could see his face. The posse thought he was Billy and shot him dead. They also shot a horse. Its dead body fell across the door of the house and blocked it.

Surrounded

Garrett's posse settled down to wait for Billy to give himself up. Billy had a sense of humor. He and Garrett joked with one another. The posse cooked up breakfast and invited the outlaws to join them. At first the men inside the building refused to give themselves up. As they grew more hungry, the smell of food became too tempting. At sundown the gang came out of the house. Billy the Kid had surrendered. Garrett let the outlaws eat the meal before he arrested them.

A DEAD HORSE

A few days after his capture, Billy gave an interview. He told a newspaper reporter: "If it hadn't been for the dead horse in the doorway, I wouldn't be here today. I would have ridden out on my bay mare and taken my chances of escaping."

Garrett and his posse deliberately tempted Billy and his gang with the smells of campfire cooking.

Betrayed Gave secret or harmful information about someone to an enemy.

Hideout A place used to hide from other people.

Escape from Jail

Billy was taken to the small town of Mesilla, New Mexico, to stand trial for the murder of Sheriff Brady.

Billy shoots his guard, Deputy Bob Olinger. The two men knew one another—and hated each other.

Billy was put on trial on April 8, 1881. He was charged with murdering two men in Lincoln County: Sheriff Brady and another member of the House posse named Buckshot Roberts. After just one day, Billy was found guilty of killing Brady. Four days later, the judge sentenced him to hang on May 13, 1881. Billy was sent back to Lincoln to be executed. He was put in **shackles** and locked in a room in the county courthouse.

Another escape

Billy did not plan to wait for his execution. A week after being put in jail, he escaped on April 28, 1881. Exactly how Billy managed to get away is unclear, but

This is another illustration of Billy's escape. He later said he did not intend to kill the guards.

he managed to shoot dead both of his guards with a gun he got from somewhere. In some stories about the escape the gun was hidden in an outhouse. Billy then removed his shackles with an ax, stole a horse and some guns, and rode out of town. Billy's reputation as a notorious outlaw was sealed forever.

GUILTY!

Billy was one of six Regulators present when Sheriff Brady was shot. It is not even certain that he fired the fatal shot. But Billy was the only man to go on trial for the murder. In fact, he was the only person to be convicted of any crime committed in the Lincoln County War.

Shackles Metal cuffs used to chain a prisoner's wrists or ankles together.

Death of Billy

Billy was on the run again. After killing the two guards, he was now the most wanted man in America.

This drawing of Billy's death shows Billy holding a gun. In fact, he was probably unarmed.

Even though there was a **bounty** on his head, Billy did not travel far. His friends urged him to go to Mexico. He would be safe from arrest there. Instead, Billy returned to the Fort Sumner area. Pat Garrett was amazed that Billy had not run farther away.

Three months after Billy's escape, Garrett and a three-man posse headed for Fort Sumner. At around midnight on July 14, 1881, Garrett and his men arrived in the town to look for Billy. Garrett asked around about the outlaw. He discovered that Billy was staying with a friend named Pete Maxwell.

Garrett gets his man

Garrett also knew Maxwell, so he headed over to Maxwell's house. What happened next is not known for sure. In one story, Billy was in bed. In another story, he had just returned from visiting a girlfriend. Both stories agree that Billy went into Maxwell's room. He may or may not have been carrying a knife. He did not know Garrett was waiting for him in the dark. As Billy entered the room he called out "Quién es? Quién es?," Spanish for "Who is it? Who is it?" Garrett fired two bullets that killed the outlaw instantly. Billy the Kid was dead, at just 21 years old.

BILLY'S FUNERAL

Almost every citizen of Fort Sumner followed the wagon that carried Billy's coffin to the cemetery. Billy was buried alongside his two friends and fellow outlaws, Tom O'Folliard and Charlie Bowdre. Later a tombstone was placed over the three graves. The single stone is carved with the names of the three men and the word *Pals*.

The tombstone still stands in Fort Sumner, but no one is sure where in the cemetery Billy's grave is located.

PALS

TOM.
O'FOLLIARD
DIED DEC. 1880

WILLIAM H.
BONNEY
ALIAS
"BILLY THE K..."
DIED JULY 1...

CHARLIE BOWDRE
DIED DEC. 1880

Bounty A sum of money paid for capturing or killing a person or an animal.

Focus: Billy's Legacy

After Billy's death, his reputation as a daring gunfighter grew. The truth was largely forgotten.

Pat Garrett's book about Billy the Kid was published in 1882.

Billy's adventures were soon being featured in dime novels and popular magazines. The stories claimed to be true, but most of them were not. Within a year of Billy's death, five books about him had been published. One was by his killer, Pat Garrett. The books depicted Billy as a heartless gunfighter. They did not explain why Billy acted as he did. They did not mention Billy's loyalty to John Tunstall or how he helped stand up against the House in Lincoln County.

Did Billy survive?

In the 1920s there was renewed interest in Billy's life and death. Since then, he has been the subject of many movies and books. Some of the books claim that Billy escaped from Pete Maxwell's house. They argued he was too good a gunman to be caught off guard. They say that Pat

Garrett must have shot another outlaw that night. Whoever Garrett shot is the man buried in Fort Sumner cemetery.

At least 20 men later claimed to be Billy. The two with the strongest claims were John Miller and Ollie Roberts. To try to solve the mystery, a plan was made in 2004 to carry out **DNA** tests. The plan failed because no one knows which grave is Billy's. So it is still possible that Billy the Kid survived.

BILLY IN NEW MEXICO

For the people of New Mexico, Billy remains a heroic figure. He helped stand up to the ranchers who ran Lincoln County. When it seemed Billy's body might be dug up in 2004, the governor of New Mexico even hired a lawyer to represent Billy's interests.

The 1988 movie *Young Guns* told the story of Billy during the Lincoln County War. Historians praised the film's accuracy.

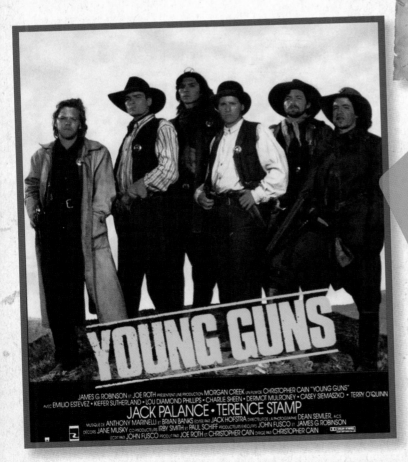

JAMES G. ROBINSON et JOE ROTH PRÉSENTENT UNE PRODUCTION MORGAN CREEK UN FILM DE CHRISTOPHER CAIN "YOUNG GUNS"
AVEC EMILIO ESTEVEZ · KIEFER SUTHERLAND · LOU DIAMOND PHILLIPS · CHARLIE SHEEN · DERMOT MULRONEY · CASEY SIEMASZKO · TERRY O'QUINN
JACK PALANCE · TERENCE STAMP DIRECTEUR DE LA PHOTOGRAPHIE DEAN SEMLER. A.C.S.
MUSIQUE DE ANTHONY MARINELLI et BRIAN BANKS ÉDITÉ PAR JACK HOFSTRA
DÉCORS DE JANE MUSKY CO-PRODUCTEURS IRBY SMITH et PAUL SCHIFF PRODUCTEURS EXÉCUTIFS JOHN FUSCO et JAMES G. ROBINSON
ÉCRIT PAR JOHN FUSCO PRODUIT PAR JOE ROTH et CHRISTOPHER CAIN DIRIGE PAR CHRISTOPHER CAIN

DNA A chemical that holds unique genetic information about a person.

ROGUES' GALLERY

Billy the Kid was just one of the outlaws in the West. Many others appeared in the most-wanted lists in the 19th century.

Tom O'Folliard
(c.1858–1880)

Tom O'Folliard was a cowboy and rustler from Texas. He became Billy the Kid's best friend. They both rode with the Regulators in the Lincoln County War. O'Folliard was shot by Pat Garrett's posse at Fort Sumner on December 19, 1880. He died soon after.

Jesse Evans
(1853–?)

Evans was a cowboy who was also a rustler. Evans recruited Billy the Kid into his gang known as "The Boys." He later went to work for Jimmy Dolan, which pitted him against Billy and the Regulators. Billy testified against Evans, who was sent to jail. There are no records of what happened to him after he served his sentence.

Wild Bill Hickok
(1837–1876)

James Butler Hickok was raised in Illinois before he joined an antislavery gang in Kansas. During the Civil War he became a police detective in Missouri. Hickok became a town marshal but was also a gambler and gunfighter. In July 1865 he shot and killed a gambler named Davis Tutt in the first known "quick-draw" gunfight. He later shot and killed a number of men who drew guns on him. Hickok was shot dead as he played cards in Deadwood, South Dakota.

Dave Rudabaugh
(1854–1886)

Dave Rudabaugh was a rustler who had been in gangs in Texas. He joined Billy's gang in New Mexico. He was arrested by Pat Garrett and sentenced to hang for shooting a deputy. He escaped but was later killed in an argument over a game of cards in a bar in Mexico.

Belle Star
(1848–1889)

Belle Star was known for her shooting and horse-riding skills and her great dress style. She was linked with the James-Younger gang. She is thought to have carried out a number of crimes but was only ever charged with horse theft. The crime was punishable by death. Instead, Belle spent nine months in jail.

GLOSSARY

Adobe Bricks made from mud dried in the sun.

Amnesty An official pardon for a crime.

Betrayed Gave secret or harmful information about someone to an enemy.

Bounty Money paid for capturing or killing a person or animal.

Branding The burning of an owner's identification mark on an animal's skin.

Court order An official order made by a judge or court.

Cylinder The rotating part of a revolver that holds the bullets.

Dime novels Cheap, popular books that usually tell very romantic or dramatic stories.

DNA A chemical that holds unique genetic information about a person.

Feuds Long and bitter quarrels.

Fictionalized Describes true stories to which details have been added to make them fiction.

Frontier The border area between settled land and the wilderness beyond.

Hideout A place used to hide from other people.

Hospitality The friendly treatment of guests, visitors, or strangers.

Immunity A promise that someone will not be punished for a crime.

Independent Governing itself.

Justice of the peace A local legal official with powers to investigate some crimes.

Pioneers The first people to settle a new region.

Posse A group of citizens helping a sheriff.

Railheads Towns where railroads join important roads or trails.

Range An open area of land where livestock can wander.

Resign To voluntarily give up a job or an official position.

Revolver A pistol with a revolving chamber to hold bullets.

Reward Money offered in return for the capture or killing of a wanted criminal.

Romantic Associated with an idealized view of reality.

Rustler Someone who steals cattle or horses.

Shackles Metal cuffs used to chain a prisoner's wrists or ankles together.

Sheriffs Officials whose job it is to enforce laws and arrest lawbreakers.

Smallholding A small property used for farming.

Terrorized Caused someone to feel fear and terror.

Tuberculosis An infectious disease that attacks the lungs and makes it difficult to breathe.

Warrants Documents authorizing an arrest.

FURTHER RESOURCES

Books

Green, Carl R., and William Sanford. *Billy the Kid.* Outlaws and Lawmen of the Wild West. Berkeley Hights, NJ: Enslow Publishers, Inc., 2008.

Murray, Stuart. *Eyewitness Wild West.* New York: DK Children, 2005.

Price, Sean. *Crooks. Cowboys, and Characters: The Wild West.* American History Through Primary Sources. Chicago, IL: Raintree Fusion, 2007.

Staton, Hilarie N. *Cowboys and the Wild West.* All About America. New York: Kingfisher, 2011

Thompson, Paul B. *Billy the Kid: "It Was a Game of Two and I Got There First."* Americans the Spirit of a Nation. Berkeley Hights, NJ: Enslow Publishers, Inc., 2010.

Woog, Adam. *Billy the Kid.* Legends of the Wild West. New York: Chelsea House Publishers, 2010.

Websites

http://www.eyewitnesstohistory.com/ billythekid.htm
An eyewitness account of Billy's death written by his killer, Sheriff Pat Garrett.

http://www.pbs.org/wgbh/ americanexperience/films/billy/player/
A PBS page supporting the documentary *Billy the Kid*, with clips from the show and many links to background information.

http://www.biography.com/people/ billy-the-kid-278971
Biography.com life of Billy the Kid, with many links.

http://www.historynet.com/billy-the-kid
A page from Historynet with a full biography of Billy, including a number of eyewitness accounts.

INDEX